Anna Saunders

Burne Jones and the Fox

Indigo Dreams Publishing

First Edition: Burne Jones and the Fox
First published in Great Britain in 2016 by:
Indigo Dreams Publishing
24, Forest Houses
Cookworthy Moor
Halwill
Beaworthy
Devon
EX21 5UU

www.indigodreams.co.uk

Anna Saunders has asserted her right under the Copyright, Designs and Patents Act 1988 to be identified as the author of this work.

ISBN 978-1-910834-16-9

British Library Cataloguing in Publication Data. A CIP record for this book can be obtained from the British Library.

Designed and typeset in Palatino Linotype by Indigo Dreams.
Cover design by Ronnie Goodyer at Indigo Dreams.
Background from print of Pan and Psyche, Edward Burne Jones.
Printed and bound in Great Britain by 4edge Ltd.
Papers used by Indigo Dreams are recyclable products made from wood grown in sustainable forests following the guidance of the Forest Stewardship Council.

For Sheila and Peter Saunders

Acknowledgements

With heartfelt thanks to The Arts Council England for awarding me a Grant For The Arts for this collection and to Lady Lever Art Gallery, Liverpool Museums for allowing me to spend many hours with their Burne Jones' paintings, and to read from the collection in the gallery space. Thank you to my friends and colleagues, too numerous to mention, who have offered me inspiration and support whilst writing the collection. With special thanks to Angela France for her editorial support and to my mother, Sheila Saunders, for textual advice given.

I'd also like to thank Ronnie and Dawn from Indigo Dreams for their encouragement and input, and for the creation of my beautiful and 'foxy' cover. And with thanks, as ever, to Nigel McLoughlin for his guidance and tuition.

Acknowledgments are also due to the following magazines and publications in which some of these poems have appeared: *New Walk Magazine, Envoi, Diamond Cutters Anthology, The North, Amaryllis and Hands and Wings*.

Also by Anna Saunders:

Kissing the She Bear, Wild Conversations Press, 2015
Struck, Pindrop Press, 2014
Communion, Wild Conversations Press, 2010

CONTENTS

'Ned' Burne Jones's love for the artist Maria Zambaco; muse and model. 9

Vulpes Vulpes 20

Dog Fox 21

Between Dog and Wolf 22

Vixen 23

Where the Wild Things are 25

Black Dog's Brown Brother 26

The Apples 27

How Watteau Would Have Painted Me 28

The Sisters 29

The Swarm 30

Public Death, Private Murder 31

The Shining 32

Missing 33

The Work 35

The Winter Visitors 36

Under the Beech Tree 37

And Now a Poem About a Garden 38

Sumbisori 39

After Daphne 40

Hazel, Honeysuckle 41

The Merlin Enters the Tower.. 42

Stolen from the Fair 43

The Forest... 44

Many 45

What Widows Eat 46

The Carpet.. 47

The Lighthouse Keeper's Daughter... 48

Captured 49

Badgers 51

Before a Blood Moon 52

Watching the Wind 53

Burne Jones and the Fox

"Hélas! Je sais un chant d'amour, triste ou gai, tour a tour."
[Alas, I know a love song, sad or happy, each in turn.]
Jules Breton, poet and painter

'Ned' Burne Jones's love for the artist Maria Zambaco; muse and model.

I

Maria is brought to the studio.

The Duchess has brought a girl
for Ned to paint.

Is this *Aglea* who is marched in,
the other two graces occupied at home?

Aphrodite's handmaiden, she sports a honeyed girdle.
All artistry, all enchantment is in that strap.

He too will wear the brace
until it proves too heavy to bear,
too tight to let him breathe.

But for now *Himeros* will burn in golden rings
around his core,
scooping out the darkness with each sun.

II

Maria sits for Ned.

He does not shape her from rock, like Pygmalion,
Instead, turns her to stone with his brush.

Hellenic beauty, *born at the base of Olympus*
she is raised to a plinth.

She will be *Summer, Venus, Nimue, Psyche,*
her face carved into their bold forms.

It is not until the final drawings that she is ephemeral.

He will sketch her then with a light pencil,
capture her in lines as slight as spider–silks.

Her eyes, encircled by pluming curls
are moons at the centre of passing cloud,

coals burning in plumes of smoke,
rocks washed over by a retreating tide.

III

Ned's wife Georgie dreams of his studio.

Georgie falls into sleep, as if into the lap of one of his models,
their plump skirts filling her ears,
muffling the sound of a chair dragged to the window
so he can *better see the hungry moon.*

The corridor of her dreams is silent.
Even with her ear against wood
she cannot hear her husband's voice entreating.

Above the waters of sleep carriages trundle past,
someone smashes a glass and Ned darkens his brush
to paint the black tendrils of the enchantress's hair.

In the studio of Georgia's dreams there are no pots
of paint, no easels, or gilt frames
buttressed against the wall.

But Maria is everywhere,
her face painted again and again

pale, gibbous, iridescent
now on the shoulders of Phyllis,
now Nimue, now Merlin.

The darkness cauterised
by a hundred pitted moons.

IV

A portrait of Maria as Psyche.

Ned paints Maria as Psyche.
Her sleeves billowing like a sea swell.

Her cold hands rest on poetry,
bones raised like the ridges of a shell.

Cupid is holding a curtain back,
to reveal a room as dark
as a thousand leagues down.

Maria's red rose is in tatters.
It lies like flotsam at her finger tips.

V

Ned portrays Maria as Venus – who marries Vulcan but falls
passionately in love with Mars.
After the painting *Venus Epithalamia*

Maria is Venus,
posed between two chambers.

At first glance she could be a Caryatid,
or a decorative pillar,
bearing the weight of the room.

She is gold-tinted, silky as a glazed vase,
lustrous as marble,

posed *contrapposto*
as if the artist were still in the room.

Light floods and illuminates her limbs
yet her face remains in shadow.

Follow the curve of her neck
and your gaze will drop like hers
so that you appear deep in thought, or despondent.

Cupid stands upon the plinth
his face obscured with a mask.

In another room garlands are hung,
the choir practise their scales.

What epithalamium for those who marry fire?

The poets sing of the betrothal
yet only the painting speaks of the inner war.

VI

*Ned paints Maria as Nimue, who has imprisoned Merlin in the
hawthorn tree.*
After the painting *The Beguiling of Merlin*

Merlin is spider-spun, strung up in the silks of a web.
Nimue has his book of tricks, is studying his sleight of hand.

The boughs above her are a swarthy needles' eye
though which she is sewn.

Ned has painted her hair like Medusa,
her black locks are serpentine.

Turn the painting on its side
and it could be Nimue latticed in the tree;

the snaking boughs entangled
with the tendrils of her hair.

All the magic in the book has been exhausted.

Its blank pages are the white wings
of a bird that cannot fly.

VII

As Ned and Maria's love become more intense, he draws on the myth of Phyllis, who is trapped in a tree until her lover's embrace frees her.
After the painting *The Tree of Forgiveness*

How long does he stand there
twisting the white wreath in his hand like a rosary?

All winter she has slept in the gnarled bark
and now she breaks into blossom with his touch.

He has one foot forward as if running,
one foot pressed back against her roots.

She is a flesh trap, a pale brace,
he writhes in her grasp like prey.

Phyllis wears the split trunk like a manacle
as they push and pull.

The earth has them fixed fast
in this coupling.

Only when it relinquishes hold
will they be free.

VIII

Like Cupid and Psyche, Maria and Ned's destinies are entangled.
After the painting *Psyche and Cupid*

Cupid's tunic plumes scarlet,
like blood swirling in water.
With a silk loop he hooks her.

He is a figure of eight,
the snake eating its own tail,
the *ouroboros* meaning infinity.

Psyche and Cupid repeat
their old arguments.

The poison is administered
then the antidote.

This will never be done.
Psyche will keep
sinking back into the underworld.

The box will lie open
at her feet. Hades will escape as smoke.

When Ned refuses to leave his wife, Maria attempts to kill herself. The Water nymph Syrinx also tried to drown herself before being turned to a pipe by Pan.
After the painting *Pan and Psyche*

Was the water Syrinx dived into too shallow,
the river drunk to a puddle by a droughty sun?

Did Syrinx wail like Cassandra before she leapt,
or the Water Nymphs turn Maria to a reed?

Was Maria too fine-spun to sink,
the goat god watch the slender stalk float?

Who scooped Maria out by a hoof,
took his lips to her?

Who manacled Syrinx on his arm,
led her into the dim streets?

What song did Pan play on Maria,
what music did he make of her?

X

Toward the end of his affair with Maria, Ned uses his wife as a model for one of his paintings.
After the painting *King Cophetua and the Beggar Maid*

At first glance this is a portrait of adoration.
Ned has painted his wife as the worshipped Maid.
The king is almost on his knees.
Pale as an absence of paint, she sits above him.

Overhead two choir boys lean into each other
as if studying the love lyrics for an epithalamium.

But look at the little flowers she is holding,
the cluster of stamens,
the yellow planets orbiting a central star.

Pale wood anemones or *Aphrodite's tears.*

Subtle stars, closed cups, their heads loll on silk,
as the shivering girl clutches at thin stalks.

Burne Jones and the Fox

Like a blood moon through a broken cloud
the fox emerges with blaze of red.

She's standing at the entrance to the scrubland
and starts backing up when she sees him,
her amber eyes supplicating.

Ned has Maria's letter crushed in his pocket.
The one in which she begs him to leave.

The gold notes in the vixen's eyes deepen
as if with disappointment, before she turns.

The fox rises from darkness each night
without danger,

but Ned is scared of the heft of stone
the rock being pushed before the door.

A tip of red, like a brush dipped in paint
is twitching, as the vixen turns.

Georgie is building a fire, turning up the gas
as Ned steps backwards toward the house.

Vulpes Vulpes

Autumn leaves lie lank as pelts
as dog and vixen circle

tails blazing like flames
forging a perfect sphere.

Cold night spikes skin,
hardens fur to stiff turf.
A blade of tail slashes the dark.

Then the knot – a barbed lock
holding them fast as they push and pull.

It is only when he withdraws
and his spikes rake that she cries out.

Her familiar scream is like silence to him.

Dog Fox

For months after it happens her strings stay taut
so when she hears a scream at 2am,
she snaps straight up and jerks at the window like a puppet.

There's no one out there – just a vixen and dog –
locked into each other in the knot.

The dog fox is alone later, outside her flat
head lowered, back dipped
so the belly almost scrapes the floor.

He's prowling close to the door
moving slowly, and with stealth.

Between Dog and Wolf

Dusk at the crossroads
and my lover is a menagerie.

Bewitched by the Fairy Queen,
the beasts within him break through.

As his skin bristles to a furze and grazes me,
his nose turns to snout,
I am fixed and tight as a hunter's brace.

Hold on, and you will save me,
a wolf with his voice says.

Slithering and spitting he is snake
then fire brand – and I throw his tongues
into the stream.

When he took me into the forest
the pine needles were rough fur
against my face.

Now his child turns within me.
Little newt suffering a sea change,
tissue turning to bone and bedrock,
of what nature we do not know.

Inspired by the ballad of Tam Lin in which a mortal captured by the fairies is transformed into a variety of beasts, and then to a stick of fire. He is rescued by a woman he has 'seduced' in the forest.

Vixen
After the novel *Lady Into Fox* by David Garnett

Turn the pages to the part in the book
when the hero wakes to find his lover
lying next to him, snout tucked under her paw

and she looks up at him with amber eyes,
irises like black planets suspended in glass.

As he strokes her scrub-grass pelt
he remembers how she'd dragged her heels at the aviary
licked her lips at the birds

how she crawled
across the room to him, peeled off his clothes
as if she were stripping the skin off a chicken,

and, later as he tried to pull away, how she'd screamed.

The Heart of Fox

*'I will rend the fox, and will eat his heart, and thus I shall become
wise'* Hebrew Fable

How shrewd is Fox to cast a tapering shadow across the waves
to look as if he is
down there; a serf in the court of the sea; *Fox Fish,* fur turned to gills,
tail flicking like a pulse, as Leviathan sleeps.

Above the rocks the Angel of Death hangs, reckoning the
creatures he's dropped in.
Now Cat floats, Dog swims in a school, Horse is buoyant as
Pegasus.
Each creature silvered and glinting as a polished coin.

But fox will not get his feet wet by sinking underneath.
Only a brown *below* for him; his are mud-hewn labyrinths,
dun catacombs embedded in cleft of rock.

How long before Leviathan wakes to an absence of Fox,
orders *lebab* for his meal ?

*Fool, don't you know the astute leave their hearts at home in the morning
before embarking on the business of the day?*

Fox will go fetch it whilst Angel waits patiently
at the den's mouth.

Darkness will fall slowly as Angel stands in kicked-up earth,
ringed round by fragments of prey.

Lebab – heart (Hebrew).

Where the Wild Things are

Through the round window of the hospital,
we watch juggernauts thunder past, dirty
as the carapaces of dung beetles.

You tell me that *things don't look right* and I say
that's down to the *distortion, the black tint.*
But why does it look like the future? You ask.

To get out, you have to press a buzzer
and the doors slide open silently like in a sci-fi flick.

There's no curvaceous broad
with alien ears, dressed in a tin foil space suit.

There's a man in with an ID badge
who wants to pat your pockets.

You're now on a Section.
The wailing keeps you awake at night
and one patient claws at the walls.

The next visit I bring you a onesie.
It's a Wolf. I say.
You reject the Mickey Mouse slippers

but climb straight into the faux fur,
scrunch your hair
into a mane and grin.

Where the wild things are, you say
as you wander off down the ward.

Black Dog's Brown Brother

The dog in your head barks
at the slightest sound,
your doctor says.

Black dog's brown brother
brings a terrified trophy kill
to twitch in your lap.

Brown dog doesn't sleep in all day like his brother.
He prowls endlessly.
Worries at shoes, barks
at the sound of steps.

The doctor suggests pills
but you don't want the dog drugged.

Hasn't he seen the bit in the film
where the robbers lob a spiked steak
so the dog is out cold whilst they loot?

All night you doze like a dog,
one eye on the door.

In another city I sleep fitfully
disturbed by scratches on wood,
a pitiful whine.

The Apples
After the painting *Original Sin* by Van Der Goes

In the black-green shadows
Adam stands stiff as a shy child forced
to play charades.

Eve bulges, blue – veined,
an iris sprouting from her sex.

Yellow-faced as if gleaming neon
a lizard with the face of a girl
peers up at heavy boughs.

The apples are dry and hard as stones.
Green as unripe tomatoes.

No sweet, rouged skin,
part cherry- red, part honeyed,
golden as the Pre-Raphaelite sun,
brilliant as *Quattrocento*.

In a cell, dark but for a blade of light
which slices through stone,
brushes lie discarded as clothes

as Van Der Goes sleeps on sackcloth,
skin bristling,

mouth watering through dreams of the flesh
which once sung on his tongue.

How Watteau Would Have Painted Me
After *The Pilgrimage to Cythera* by Jean Antoine Watteau

Which one am I? I ask
when you tell me I have the look
of one of Watteau's models.

Am I am the one drowning in pooling silk,
crouched at the base of a sword?

Or the woman being offered smashed flower buds
as if they were coins?

All the models are close to the shrine,
posed near the feet of the Goddess of Love.

Each couple are petals – linked like the roses
which necklace Venus's neck.

I thought the afternoon would last longer.
We had barely arrived
but already it was time to go.

Is that me, with the man who raises to tiptoes
as if to run
even while he is nuzzling?

No, I see myself now; the girl in an embrace
which forces her back to the boat.

That's me; the one who offers a silent plea to Venus,
as if an effigy could turn time into stone.

Some have read The Pilgrimage to Cythera, as the arrival of lovers to a
shrine of Venus. But it depicts their departure.

The Sisters

The horses have the look of girls in Dutch Masters,
their heads dropped demurely
as if doing needlepoint.

Stock-still they stand,
eyes averted to the ground,
backs weighted down by livery.

In the darkness their hide is luminous
as a communion dress.

The man sitting on top of the box
pulls the reins taut.
They are decent stock, he says, *sisters.*

They know not to bare their teeth
or raise their heads suddenly
when braying men spill out of the pub.

They are good girls, the driver says,
the whip lying lank at his feet.

The Swarm

The sand is stained scarlet as if a vein had emptied,
a blood spill made up of a seething mass
of beetles, each insect a single cell.

She watches bathers screaming
as they leap from the red waters ,
sees small children covered
in wiggling shells.

Later she will call it a *plague*
shudder when she speaks of it,

talk *sotto voce* of how the bugs
clung to her, leeching the sweat
from her skin.

She will have forgotten it by the time
she leaves home, and years later
cleaning her flat

they will just look like tacks toppled
from the wall or old pennies –
until they rock themselves upright.

A scarlet shell landing on her bed
as shocking as puberty's sudden show.

After the ladybird plague of 1976.

Public Death, Private Murder

Brash with gaudy tales he'd blazed
into the bar, skin tanned truffle-dark.

He'd taunted our lads for doffing caps,
for plodding, manacled with mud,
slack-shouldered as cattle in harness.

He didn't need a lamp he said,
had gone singing into the storm.
Who knew he'd be followed?

They'd crashed tattered limbs like wings,
left him shedding scarlet berries on the snow.

We'd not answer questions,
give names, we'd meet the police with silence.

Yet like baby blackbirds,
feeding from the adults golden *gape*
we took the story from mouth to mouth,

dissolved it with silvered juices
until each and every one of us wore it on the tongue.

*After the chapter in Cider with Rosie by Laurie Lee in which the village closes
ranks after a murder is committed.*

The Shining

We'd never call them that now, but back then
when their dirty-halo eyes
and matching baby doll dresses
called out for it, we'd yell *The Grady Twins!* and run.

Come play with us…for ever!
we'd shout, hyped up after watching
the bit where the boy has peddled on his little red bike
down the hall and *they* are standing there
fingers latticed, unblinking.

Eight years old and they have the eyes
of old men released from Auschwitz.

There will be blood pooling
beneath a lift door. A man embracing
bones. The boy will have somebody dead
to talk to.

None of us believe that it's possible
to see the future
and we wonder why it's called *The Gift.*

I'm shining! We shriek.

Who saw the signs?
The bruises beneath their mother's eyes.
The police cars clustered
outside their house.
The father led out in cuffs.

Missing

There's no evidence as such,
but other drinkers may recall a couple
huddled in the snug, colour rising
in the woman's face
as the flames licked it to a red welt.

The barmaid – distracted by the moon,
a molar-white snarl through cloud,
would have missed seeing them sneak

into the yard by the church,
and, turning to the drouthy man raising his glass,
would have put them out of mind.

After that then there's nothing to be heard
except a vixen-like cry raking the air,
the hiss of a cat prowling in the grass
bridling at the sight of red.

Nothing, no clues. Not when the single Rizla
carrying skin cells
is blown into the bushes by the same ravening wind
that gusts the blades back up.

And then the rain,
coming down like hands in absolution
hurrying a single blonde hair into the gutter,
washing a print from a grave.

No one has reported a crime, yet surely something is amiss?

For days after, a phone is lifted again and again

as if someone were checking the line

a face emerges through curtains
like that same hungry moon

and a woman in a double bed turns and turns
like someone so ravenous they cannot sleep.

The Work

The slow breath of a god has inscribed the sky.

A plumed, white exhalation
drawn-out as a sigh of appreciation
for the waves

for the yolk-bright blooms of ragwort,
the sloughing ferns,

the orbs of reflected sun,
which morph like blown glass
in the oxbow pools.

This, suggests the shore, is the hand of an artist.

The strawberry clovers nod their heads
in affirmation and the waves sibilance
is an insistent *yes.*

Whose signature is that
in the black seaweeds scribble?
Who has signed their name in the sands?

The Winter Visitors

The winter visitors mass around the water,
populating it like shingle.

From here they could be oyster shells
splitting carapaces to birth pearls.

Come closer and you will see their dun wings
open to reveal the white beneath.

The horses which stand in the same, waterlogged, field
have their eyes closed.

How peaceful they look
sleeping amongst such flux

heads hanging down as if listening intently
to all the waders have to say –

about the changing of the seasons, perhaps
or how to read the turn.

The birds will drop their beaks back down
and hover them like divining rods.

The leaves that have hoarded their sugars deepen to red.
In the blackberry bush autumn ripens its dark.

Under the Beech Tree

We circle the gallows, watch as grizzling saws
gnaw at each limb.

Under each bitten off bough is a gleaming whorl,
a bright concentric circle new born, brilliant pink.

The shrieking teeth turn the beech to totem, to temple pillar.

Old Red has stood over us for two hundred years.
We've lain in the black lake of its shadows,
scampered like squirrels over its roots.

Gnarled god, with open arms, now its dust
falls, to anoint us.

And Now a Poem About a Garden
For Frankie and Kathy

The curtain swags are as glossy and ruched
as roses pined back on a stake
and the chandeliers' silver roots
dangle into the air.

We nestle in our seats,
neat and bright as bedding plants.

As night amasses in the glass
the bright petals of each poem open.

The actress reads a line
by Marvell,
her voice is a bee's soft drone.

The blooms of the hibiscus
are closing to seal in their scent
from the dark.

We open our corollas,
extend stamens,
as if under the bright morning sun.

Sumbisori

The waves swell
like bodies pulvinated with flesh.

The women watch the sea flex its muscles
before they leap.

Their rubber suits
bob before they go down.

Eel-black, seal-smooth
one-by-one they go under.

What are they looking for, down there?
Lobsters? Coral?

Their hands grope for spoil
as they glide.

There is only so long a woman can stay down
before she'll break the surface with a sigh.

But before that
the trill,
the quick intake of breath.

Then, to empty the lungs
the Sumbisori
that they learnt from the seals.

An exhalation,
half high-pitched scream
half wolf-whistle for the waves.

After Daphne

He told me my hands were smooth
as soap-stone, that hers were callused,
shredded by nights spent working wood,
whittling branches to blades, carving a flint from stick.

He told me her nails were like *Blood Moons*,
that he'd seen her skinning a rabbit
as if she were pulling the dress off a doll.

I'm to blame for taking him by the river.
How was I to know where it would lead?

Later he picked bark out of his clothes,
yellow flowers from his hair,

fashioned a wreath of long green leaves,
and begged me to wear it.

Hazel, Honeysuckle

I
Embroidered rugs cover the floor of the castle.

At night Isolde peels them back,
presses her spine against stone.

dreams of the clammy rock,
the hot dark of the cave,

Tristan's fingers sticking to her hair, glistening
with the skinned flesh of rabbit.

King Mark's hands are mollusc-soft.
In the Royal bed they make sweetmeats of her.

II
Tristan plucks a love lyric from his harp.

Rising notes stumble into silence as a poisoned dart
pierces his skin.

The sea's faltering chorus sings *Tristan, Tristan*.

III
The soil is scooped open to insert Tristan's body.
Isolde beats the ground, desperate to join him under the earth.

IV
A suckering shrub entangles an arching vine,
peach and white thread evergreen.

Stems bind boughs, sew honeysuckle to hazel.
Who knows where one limb begins, the other ends.

The Merlin Enters the Tower

As bird of prey the Fairy King is feathered.
He flies in jessed and hooded, puffs a rufous chest.

He's sick, he says, of being a plumy jewel on a Lady's hand.

As Merlin he can mimic the Mistle Thrush,
as Fairy King he can ape her shape.

Call me Jack, he says with *her* mouth,
before his lips elongate to beak.

She'd watched his rusty buff, his storm-sky rump,
had savoured his elfin falsetto as he hung on the wind.

He'll be gentle as a dove, he says,
as his talons pick stitches from her robe.

Later, her husband curses himself for raising her to the sky
and, hearing a scratch and skitter
but knowing there are no mice,
breaks a plane of glass to a blade.

Stolen from the Fair

Anemone, how you bloom,
curves flattened by glass.

Small fruit,
what tiny fingers pushed you down?

Skinned and scooped out,
suspended in spirit and time.
My sweet *Pickled Punk*.

Sealed delicacy,
swaying in syrup,
above you a sky of tin.

My jacket swells.
I stroke my bulge.

My peach boy is washed out.
The gin took him from me.

I clasp a chill jar
against my heart.
This one will not spill.

*A 'pickled punk' is the term used by American carnival staff for preserved
foetuses, used as sideshow attractions.*

The Forest

Forget how your father hacked down the saplings,
our forest still sings
the ferns' coiled notes are quavers.

Put from your mind how your father passed the axe to you.

How he taught you to grip the handle
so the weight of the blade didn't topple you.

The firs which grew through us like spines
lattice the sky with bark and needle.

This is our darkness. It is emerald black.
The sky flashes purple.

The wild garlic's libretto is intoxicating,
and rough-tongued as lust.

The trunks you swung at still stand.

Many

You tell me how having multiple personalities is like
when five horses, roped to a holding pole,
pull in different directions.

Emma, Helen, Claire, Alice and Sue are on the phone!
My father says.

There's no gaggle of girls, no cacophony of sequels
and giggles, just a single voice.
Which one has broken free this time?

It's you – explaining how it began.

*When the lion comes down from the hills
the herd scatters*, you say.

The pole creaks and groans.
Something gives way.

What Widows Eat

Since the death she's scooped out
chunks of white bread, spooned in sugar,

eaten the concoction in bed,
keeping her eyes off the impression his body has left.

First mouthful has her tongue tingling
and she'll close her eyes as the sugar beats its wings.

She won't look at the dip
which once cupped his body
as the sweetness rushes through blood and brain.

The moon in the night sky is a silver spoon
glinting, as she sprinkles trampled stars
into an aching hollow of white.

The Carpet

Let time be a carpet
and I will pull its frayed edge towards me
carefully, so its furniture doesn't topple.

There's that white-cold china sink
the cupboards filled with bags of flour,

your little hand reaching up,
body faltering on the stool.

There's the red tin, lid removed.
Your raw-scrubbed face peering in
at the thick icing, the glossy cherry,
the scarlet band through the sponge.

The cake is the whole, round earth
with not a slice taken out yet
and your appetite is enormous.

I will pull you towards me, my father at ten,
the worn scraps beneath your feet
the years which kept me from meeting you.

I drag the rug towards me.
Look, nothing falls down.

The Lighthouse Keeper's Daughter

Custodian of the ocean's metronome
he keeps the light alive with little acts;

feeds in fuel, sparks the wicks,
opens the locks so the lens will spin.

When his daughter's time comes
to live in the white eye

she'll need a light touch
to wipe a fog from the stars

a steady hand to cast a beam
upon the turbulent sea.

Alone in the lantern room,
it will be the father's eye
that reads the storm

as she shines a ray on black waters
and guides lost travellers home.

Captured

He hawked the story round the school;
how, a half- furlong ahead of the vet,
his dad bombed down the beach

and. as if the shore were the pitch
he spent each Saturday mired in,
he rugby-tackled the animal.

He'd no fear of those spiked paws.
No worse than pinning down a scraping lass
fresh from the nail bar, he'd said.

You have to act quick with them that resist
arrest – even wallabies escaped from the zoo.

I say nothing of how my dad, *the Hack,*
stumbled as to handicap himself,
and let the creature run free.

How his ink took in the scene;
the two pensioners lagged like boilers
the steel flask – a spent bullet at their feet,
the candy stripe of their seats.

His pen had it all; how plod's helmet fell off
in the rush, how the wings of his coat
beat behind him, the scoops in sand
left from his size tens
little tombs carved out of the shore.

Yes, plod had brought the animal down,
held it in his arms, a wild
small creature thrashing,

but who had captured the pink underside
of its paws, the black billowing clouds,
the sea rolling in, who had captured the whole day?

Badgers

We almost miss what looks like a junked rug
with a black trim, heaped on the side of the road.

The badger is coiled foetal, harlequin face
tucked under a paw, white lines
running over its head like road markings, pale belly
peppered with stones.

It's still breathing, and dad calls wildlife rescue,
as we wait by the animal, pat its springy fur.

Dehydration we are told later,
The roads a desert if you're wearing fur.
In the background we hear the badger scampering.

The next family holiday we see another -
opened up as if for heart surgery,
glossy red ribbons spilling out onto the road.

My dad makes another call and the soft body,
an arrow to the sett, is removed
before the badger baiters can bring their dogs
to make sport with the animals that remain.

I only remember this, years later, the same night
I see a fleshy mound on the side of the road,
a glistening snout, a small paw protruding
like a hand reaching out for alms.
A badger, I think, briefly, without slowing down.

Before a Blood Moon
For PW

One of the musicians plays a requiem
for an astronomer father.

The room is hushed as a forest before a storm,
and his light finger-work is the start of rain

each plucked string a grass blade
trembling under first drops.

As the room grows dark
a full moon haunts the sky
like a persistent ghost.

The next song is called *Canto De Luna*.

The chords are amplified by the emptiness
at the heart of the guitar.

The guitar's hole is a dark planet
rung-round
by a carved corolla.

After the music finishes
they discuss the meaning of the *sanguis lunaris*
whilst the full moon
watches over them like parent.

Why would anyone believe in the end of the world?
someone says, laughing,
and they talk of things that never end
like circles, like love.

Watching the Wind

On the next bench, the young couple
merge into each other like clouds.

We turn away and watch the storm
bearing down upon the lake.

The gust puckers the skin,
ruches it up into accordion pleats.

White carriages of the sky roll by.
The horses that pull their cargo are invisible.

The girl blushes as she gazes at the boy.
A hidden emotion made visible in her flesh.

Something, out of sight, is flowing.

We cannot see the air currents that carry the gulls,
but we can watch the birds on them, gliding.

Indigo Dreams Publishing Ltd
24, Forest Houses
Cookworthy Moor
Halwill
Beaworthy
Devon
EX21 5UU
www.indigodreams.co.uk